The Ultimate Self-Teaching Method!

P9-CDC-778

Play Guitar Today!

A Complete Guide to the Basics

by Jeff Schroedl and Doug Downing

Recording Credits:
Todd Greene, Producer
Jake Johnson, Engineer
Doug Boduch, Guitar
Scott Schroedl, Drums
Tom McGirr, Bass
Warren Wiegratz, Keyboards
Andy Dress, Narration

ISBN 978-0-634-00410-0

HAL•LEONARD®
CORPORATION

7777 W. BLUEMOUND RD. P.O. BOX 13819 MILWAUKEE, WI 53213

Visit Hal Leonard Online at
www.halleonard.com

Introduction

Welcome to *Play Guitar Today!*—the series designed to prepare you for any style of guitar playing, from rock to blues to jazz to classical. Whatever your taste in music, *Play Guitar Today!* will give you the start you need.

About the CD

It's easy and fun to play guitar, and the accompanying CD will make your learning even more enjoyable, as we take you step by step through each lesson and play each song along with a full band. Much like with a real lesson, the best way to learn this material is to read and practice a while first on your own, then listen to the CD. With *Play Guitar Today!*, you can learn at your own pace. If there is ever something that you don't quite understand the first time through, go back on the CD and listen again. Every musical track has been given a track number, so if you want to practice a song again, you can find it right away.

Contents

Lesson 1—The Basics. 3
    The Parts of the Guitar. 3
    How to Hold Your Guitar 3
    Your Right and Left Hands 4
    Playing is Easy 4
    Tuning Up. 5
    How to Read Music 6

Lesson 2—The First String: E 7

Lesson 3—The Second String: B. 10

Lesson 4—The Third String: G 14

Lesson 5—The Fourth String: D 18

Lesson 6—The Fifth String: A. 24

Lesson 7—The Sixth String: E. 27

Lesson 8—More Notes: B♭ and E♭ 31

Lesson 9—Major Chords 35

Lesson 10—Minor Chords. 39

Lesson 11—One More Note: A 44

Lesson 12—Power Chords 46

Review. 48

The Basics

Track 1

The Parts of the Guitar

The guitar has been a popular instrument for hundreds of years because it is both versatile and portable—not to mention it sounds great!

Although there are many different kinds of guitars, they all fall into one of two basic categories: *acoustic* or *electric*. These two types are shown to the right. Find the one that most resembles your own guitar, and get acquainted with its parts.

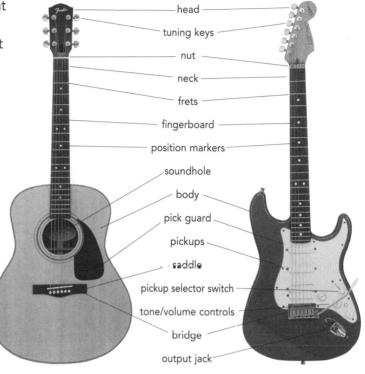

head
tuning keys
nut
neck
frets
fingerboard
position markers
soundhole
body
pick guard
pickups
saddle
pickup selector switch
tone/volume controls
bridge
output jack

acoustic   electric

Track 2

How to Hold Your Guitar

Sitting is probably the most comfortable position when first learning to play. Rest the guitar on your right thigh and hold it against the right side of your chest with your right arm. If you want to raise the neck to a more comfortable position, cross your legs—or find yourself a foot rest.

If your guitar has a strap, you may prefer to stand. The basic position of the guitar should remain the same. Your hands must always be free to move across the strings. Therefore, don't hold the guitar with your hands; support it with your body or with a strap.

Your Right and Left Hands

When you play, you'll be striking the strings with a pick held in your right hand. To hold the pick properly, grip it between the thumb and index finger, keeping the rest of your hand relaxed and your fingers curved. The fingers not holding the pick may rest on the guitar for extra support.

Your left hand belongs on the neck of the guitar. It, too, should be relaxed. To help you get a feel for the correct hand placement, follow these suggestions:

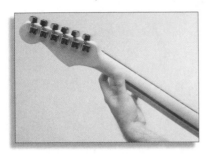

1. Place your thumb on the underside of the guitar neck.

2. Arch your fingers so that you will be able to reach all the strings more easily.

3. Avoid letting the palm of your hand touch the neck of the guitar.

Playing is Easy

You produce sounds on your guitar either by **strumming** several strings at once or by **picking** one string at a time. Take a minute to get a feel for this. With the pick in your right hand, use a downward motion and gently strum the strings. Practice this several times to get the feel of the pick and the strings. Then try picking the strings one at a time from bottom to top .

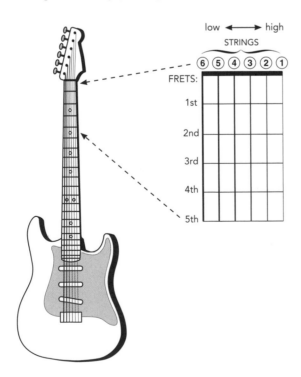

Notice that some strings sound higher and some sound lower? Each has a different **pitch**. Pitch is the highness or lowness of a sound. On the guitar, the strings are numbered 1 through 6, from the highest-sounding string (the thinnest) to the lowest-sounding one (the thickest).

As you can see, the frets of the guitar are also numbered, from low (near the nut) to high (near the bridge). Fretting higher up the neck produces sounds of a higher pitch, fretting lower on the neck produces sounds of a lower pitch.

The fingers of your left hand are also numbered, for convenience:

4

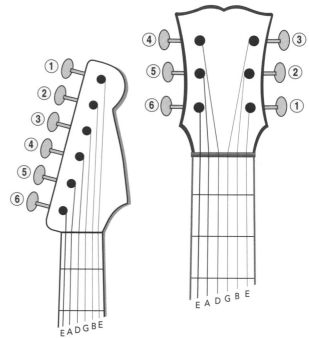

Tuning Up

If you loosen a string by turning its tuning key, the pitch will become lower; if you tighten the string, the pitch will become higher. When two pitches sound exactly the same, they are said to be *in tune*. There are many ways to get your guitar in tune: you may use an electronic tuner, a piano, a pitch pipe, a tuning fork—you can even tune your guitar purely to itself. For now, however, listen to the audio to help you tune your instrument. The guitar's six open strings should be tuned to these pitches:

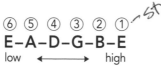

⑥ ⑤ ④ ③ ② ①—*string*
E–A–D–G–B–E
low ⟷ high

Here are a few tips to help get you started:

- Whether tightening or loosening a string, turn the peg slowly so that you can concentrate on the changes in pitch. You may need to pick the string repeatedly to compare it.

- As you're tuning a string, you may notice that a series of pulsating **beat waves** becomes audible. These beat waves can actually help you tune: they'll slow down as you get closer to bringing two pitches together, and they'll stop completely once the two pitches are exactly the same.

- Instead of tuning a string down to pitch, tune it up. Tuning up allows you to stretch the string into place, which will help it stay in tune longer. So, if you begin with a string that is too high in pitch, tune it down first, and then bring it back up to pitch.

Another Way to Tune Your Guitar

1. Tune the 6th string E to a piano, a pitch pipe, an electronic tuner, or the CD. If none of these is available, approximate E as best you can.
2. Press the 6th string at the 5th fret. This is A. Tune the open 5th string to this pitch.
3. Press the 5th string at the 5th fret. This is D. Tune the open 4th string to this pitch.
4. Press the 4th string at the 5th fret. This is G. Tune the open 3rd string to this pitch.
5. Press the 3rd string at the 4th fret. This is B. Tune the open 2nd string to this pitch.
6. Press the 2nd string at the 5th fret. This is E. Tune the open 1st string to this pitch.

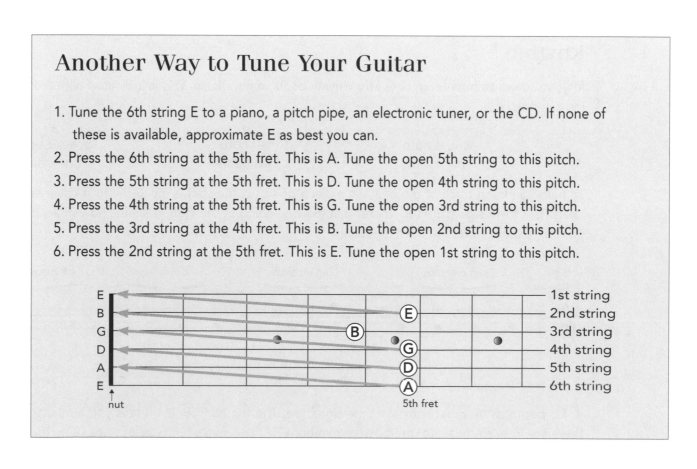

How to Read Music

Musical sounds are indicated by symbols called **notes**. Notes come in all shapes and sizes, but every note has two important components: pitch and rhythm.

Pitch

Pitch (the highness or lowness of a note) is indicated by the placement of the note on a **staff**, a set of five lines and four spaces. Notes higher on the staff are higher in pitch; notes lower on the staff are lower in pitch.

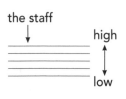

To name the notes on the staff, we use the first seven letters of the alphabet: **A–B–C–D–E–F–G**. Adding a **treble clef** assigns a particular note name to each line and space on the staff, centered around the pitch G, the second line of the staff.

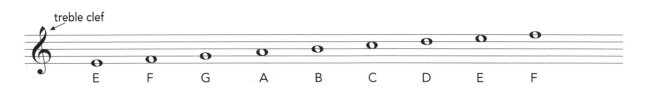

An easy way to remember the pitches on the lines is "**E**very **G**ood **B**oy **D**oes **F**ine." For the spaces, spell "FACE."

Rhythm

Rhythm refers to how long, or for how many beats, a note lasts. This is indicated with the following symbols:

whole note	half note	quarter note
(four beats)	*(two beats)*	*(one beat)*

To help you keep track of the beats in a piece of music, the staff is divided into **measures** (or "bars"). A **time signature** (or "meter") at the beginning of the staff indicates how many beats you can expect to find in each measure.

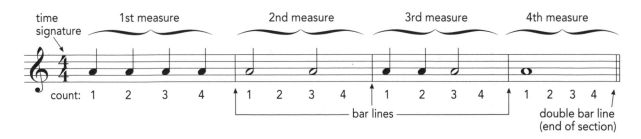

4/4 is perhaps the most common time signature. The top number ("4") tells you how many beats there are in each measure; the bottom number ("4") tells you what type of note value receives one beat. In 4/4 time, there are four beats in each measure, and each beat is worth one quarter note.

Foothill
Music 15 A – Guitar 1
2 Units

Dr. Josh Di Chiacchio
joshdichi@gmail.com
dichiacchiojoshua@fhda.edu

Required Text: Play Guitar Today Level 1 with CD By Hal Leonard Publishing.
Other handouts will be given/assigned as needed.

Student Learning Outcomes -

- The successful student will be able to apply music theory as they perform beginning fingerpicking styles and categorize chords into primary and secondary triads.
- Successful students will be able to make a comparison of folk and pop melodies based on an understanding of beginning right and left hand techniques.

Description -

A performance based course in beginning guitar (nylon, steel, or electric guitar) with a concentration on folk music. Traditional and popular songs will be used to demonstrate the development of right and left hand techniques. Standard music notation, tablature, and chord symbols will be presented and students can choose instrumental or popular vocal selections to play.

Course Objectives -

The student will be able to:

A.   Apply the fundamentals of music theory as they relate to the guitar.
B.   Demonstrate an understanding of primary chord positions (I-IV-V) in C, G, D, A, & E.
C.   Analyze the form and structure of contemporary and traditional popular songs.
D.   Demonstrate strumming and finger-style techniques for folk and popluar song accompaniment.
E.   Memorize musical notation for the guitar (tablature, chord diagrams and standard notation).
F.   Practice how to change chords rhythmically using different meters.
G.   Examine left hand technique (alternating bass, hammering-on, pulling off, and bass runs)
H.   Examine right hand technique (strumming, arpeggios, and finger picking).
I.   Compare the contributions made in the guitar repertoire from people of diverse backgrounds and cultures with changes in technology.

E-mail me prior to any absence. More than three absences will be detrimental to your grade. Late work is not accepted. Missed quizzes and exams cannot be made up. If you require any extra assistance please notify me. Office hours are available by appointment. No recording of any kind is allowed in class. Please let me know if you require extra assistance. You are expected to participate and ask questions to clarify the material. Missing class is not a valid reason for missing material. Please exchange e-mails with other students and   e-mail them if you miss an assignment. The last day to drop without a W is 10/09. The last day to drop with a W is 11/18. The following will be used to determine grades. You are expected to show up to class on time. If you are late, you will miss important information and not be given the full class period on test days.

A=100%-90%   B=89%-80%   C=79%-70%   D=69%-60%   F=59%-0%

1 string per week
17 strings
he recommends nylon string to get started.

The First String: E

The first three notes we'll learn on the guitar are all found on the high E string.

E

■ Your first note, E, is an "open-string" tone. There's nothing to fret—simply strike the open first string with your pick.

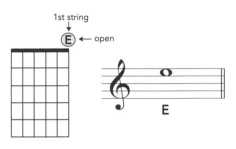

F

► Notice that your finger actually belongs *directly behind each fret.* If you place it on top of the fret, or too far back, you'll have difficulty getting a full, clear sound.

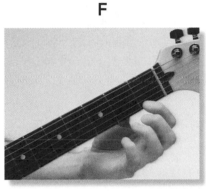

■ For the next note F, place your *first finger* on the first string directly behind the first fret, and strike the string with your pick.

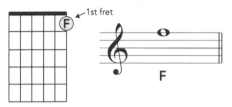

G

■ To play the note G, place your *third finger* on the first string directly behind the third fret, and strike the string with your pick.

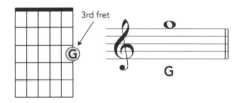

Learn to recognize these notes both on the fretboard *and* on the staff. Then, when you're comfortable playing the notes individually, try this short exercise. Speak the note names aloud as you play (e.g., "E, F, G, F...).

E–F–G

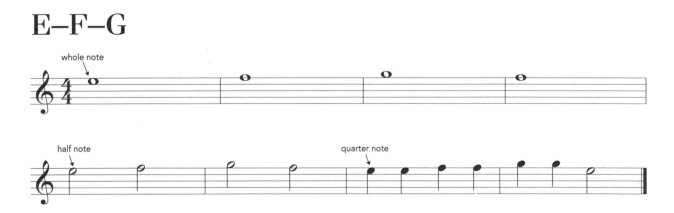

7

Of course, the best way to really learn these notes is to use them in some tunes. So let's do it. Start slowly with the following melodies, and concentrate on keeping your tempo nice and even. Practice these several times on your own before you try playing along with the audio.

Track 6

First Song

[handwritten notes: What note is this? How do you play it?]
[handwritten notes: E, 1/4 notes, 1 count, F, G, 1/2 notes get 2 counts, G]

[handwritten notes in left margin:]
e = open
F = First Finger, First Fret
G = 3rd Finger, 3rd Fret

Keeping Time

Having trouble keeping a steady rhythm? Try *tapping* and *counting* along with each song. If the guitar is resting on your right leg, use your left foot to tap. Each time the foot comes down marks one beat. In 4/4 time, tap your foot four times in each measure, and count "1, 2, 3, 4." The first beat of each measure should be accented slightly—this is indicated below by the symbol ">."

count and tap: 1   2   3   4   1   2   3   4   1   2   3   4   1   2   3   4

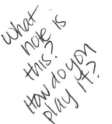
Track 7

Second Song

► If you like, read through each song *without* your guitar at first: Tap the beat with your foot, count out loud, and *clap* through the rhythms.

Track 8

Third Song

[handwritten note: 4 counts]

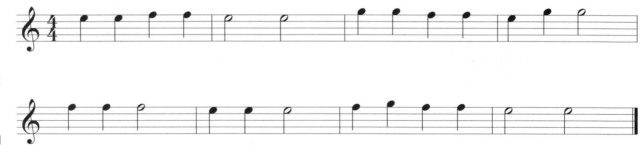

8

CHORD CHART

In this chart you will find the chords learned in this book as well as several other common chords you may see in music you are playing.

Am (nor)

x o   o

```
| | | | ①
| ② ③ | |
```

A

x o   o

```
| | | | |
| ① ② ③ |
```

A7

x o   o   o

```
| | | | |
| ① | ② |
```

B7

x   o

```
| ① | | |
② | ③ | ④
```

C

x o   o

```
| | | | ①
| | ② | |
③ | | | |
```

C7

x   o

```
| | | | ①
| | ② | |
| ③ | ④ |
```

Dm

x x o

```
| | | | ①
| | ② | |
| | | ③ |
```

D

x x o

```
| | | | |
| | ① | ②
| | | ③ |
```

D7

x x o

```
| | | | ①
| | ② | ③
```

Em

o   o o o

```
| | | | |
② ③ | | |
```

E

o   o o

```
| | | ① |
② ③ | | |
```

E7

o   o   o o

```
| | | ① |
| ② | | |
```

F

x x

```
| | | ① ①
| | ② | |
| | | ③ |
```

G

o o o

```
| | | | |
| ② | | |
③ | | | ④
```

G7

o o o

```
| | | | ①
| ② | | |
③ | | | |
```

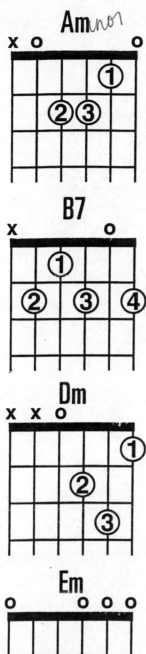
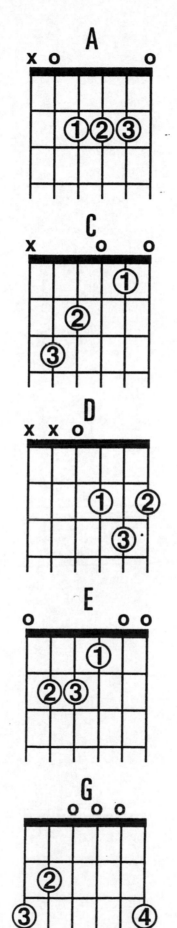
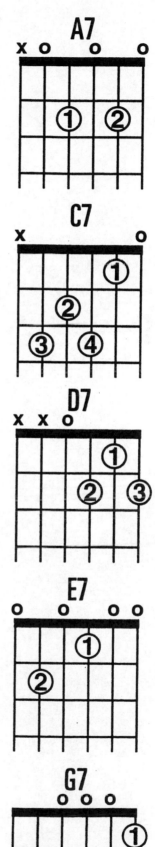

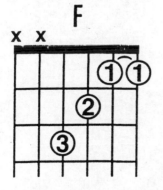

Even though you don't actually use your left hand to fret the open string E, keep that hand on the guitar in "ready position," with your thumb on the back of the neck. This will allow you to fret the other notes that much more quickly.

Track 9

Three-Note Rock

Track 10

Spiraling Downward

► Try to keep your eyes on the page, instead of on your guitar.

Picking with Downstrokes

Remember, you should be striking the strings with a *downward* motion of your pick. This is called a *downstroke*, and is sometimes indicated with the symbol ⊓.

As you play through these tunes, strive for efficiency and relaxation in your right-hand picking motion. It doesn't take much movement to get a good, solid downstroke.

before stroke

after stroke

The Second String: B

Track 11

Your next three notes are all played on the second string, B. You might want to check your tuning on that string before going any further.

B

► Notice that we're using the same fret positions as on the E string: open, 1st, and 3rd.

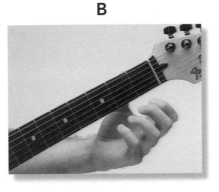

■ To play the note B, just strike the open second string.

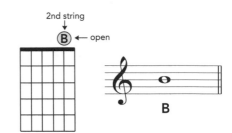

C

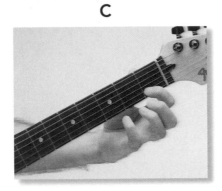

■ To play the note C, place your first finger on the second string directly behind the first fret.

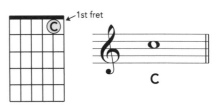

D

■ To play the note D, place your third finger on the second string directly behind the third fret.

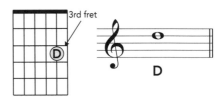

Practice these next exercises several times, slow and easy. Then play them along with the audio.

Track 12

B-C-D

TIP: Be sure to keep your left-hand fingers curved but relaxed, and use just your fingertips to fret the notes. Here's a test: you should be able to play any note on the B string, without muffling the open E above it. If you can't do this, you're probably laying your fingers too flat across the fretboard.

Track 13

Three to Get Ready

Now here are some tunes to practice all six notes you've learned so far. Don't be afraid to review E, F, and G again before tackling these!

Track 14

Two-String Rock

Fingering Tip

When moving from a lower note to a higher note on the same string, try leaving the lower note depressed. For example, on the first string, leave your first finger on F while you put your third finger on G. Now, to go back to F, you simply lift your third finger. This way, you don't have to find the first fret all over again—you're already there!

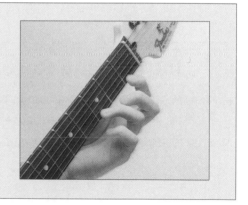

Track 15

Ode to Joy

Jingle Bells

Black Dog Blues

► This song moves from string to string a lot. Be careful and start slowly.

Introducing Rests

In addition to notes, songs may also contain silences, or *rests*—beats in which you play nothing at all. A rest is a musical pause. Rests are like notes in that they have their own rhythmic values, instructing you how long (or for how many beats) to pause:

whole rest	half rest	quarter rest
(four beats)	(two beats)	(one beat)

Try tapping, counting, and playing this exercise.

Rest Easy

Here's something else to consider: When you encounter a rest, you may need to stop any previous notes from sounding. To do this, try the following:

- For an open-string note, like E, touch the string lightly with your left-hand finger(s).
- For a fretted note, like F, decrease the pressure of your left-hand finger on the string.

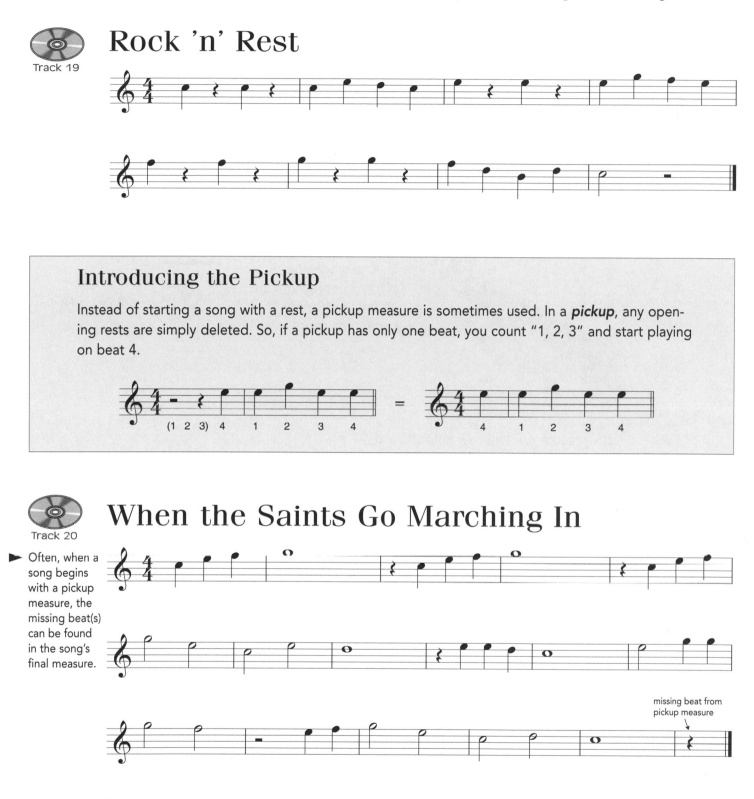

Rock 'n' Rest

Track 19

Introducing the Pickup

Instead of starting a song with a rest, a *pickup* measure is sometimes used. In a ***pickup***, any opening rests are simply deleted. So, if a pickup has only one beat, you count "1, 2, 3" and start playing on beat 4.

When the Saints Go Marching In

Track 20

Often, when a song begins with a pickup measure, the missing beat(s) can be found in the song's final measure.

missing beat from pickup measure

By the way, it's much better to practice just a little every day than it is to cram everything into one long session—your fingers and your mind need time to develop.

The Third String: G

Track 21

For this string, we'll learn just two notes, including one that's on the second fret. Don't forget to check your tuning.

G

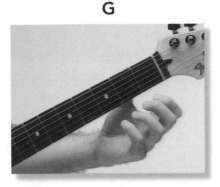

▶ Notice that we're learning another G note—since the musical alphabet contains only the letters A through G, this type of repetition will eventually occur with all the note names.

■ To play the note G, strike the open third string.

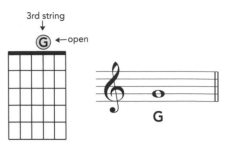

A

■ To play the note A, place your second finger on the third string, behind the second fret.

Let's practice our two new notes, G and A.

Track 22

Two-Note Jam

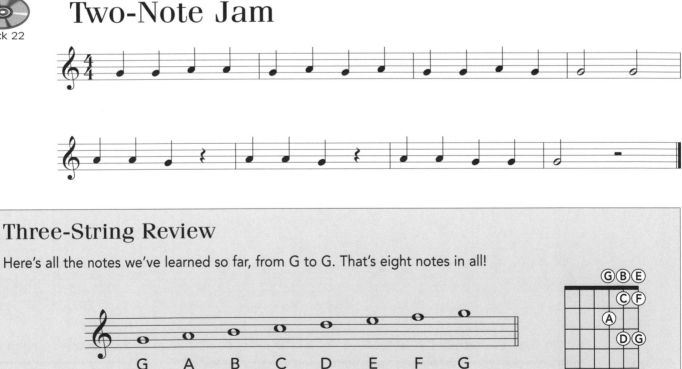

Three-String Review

Here's all the notes we've learned so far, from G to G. That's eight notes in all!

G A B C D E F G

Play through these, then play just the low G and the high G, and notice how similar they sound. Two different notes with the same letter name like this are called *octaves*. The prefix "oct" comes from the Latin word for "eight."

Remember to practice these next songs slowly at first. Ideally, you should be able to read and play the notes in time, without having to slow down or stop in the middle of a song. Speed up the tempo as you become more confident with the notes, and then play along with the band.

Brother John

Track 23

Red River Rock

Track 24

▶ Notice the pickup measure on this song. You actually begin playing on beat 3.

Aura Lee

Track 25

▶ Try this: put your guitar down and just recite the note names of the song ("G, C, B, C, D, A, D...").

Michael, Row Your Boat Ashore

Track 26

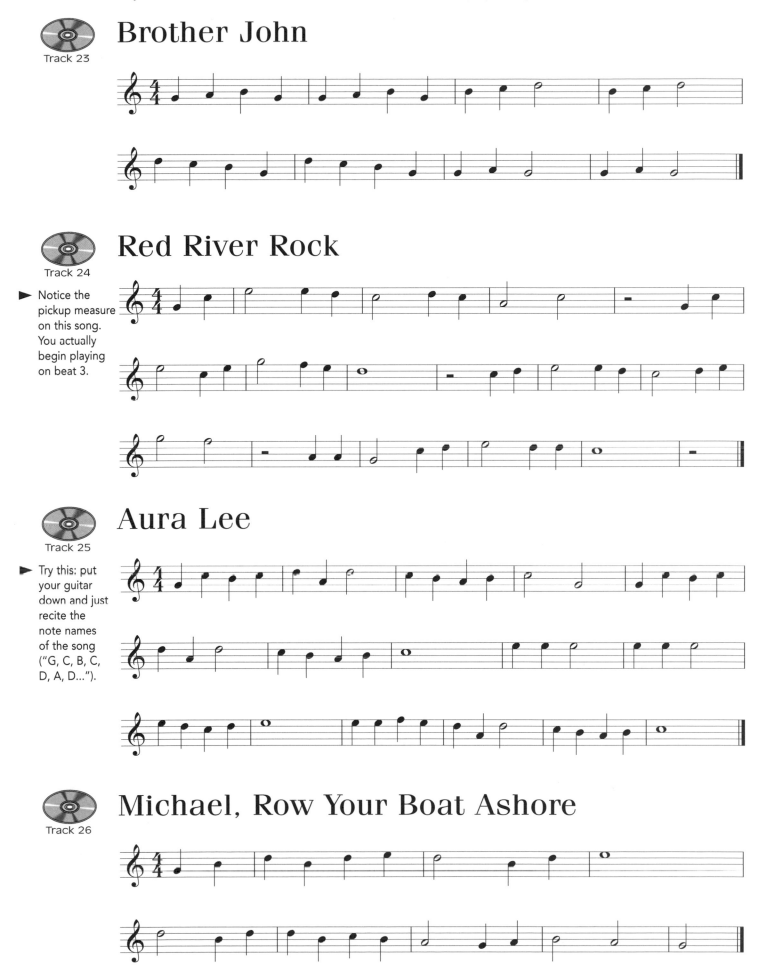

Here Comes the Guitarist

Track 27

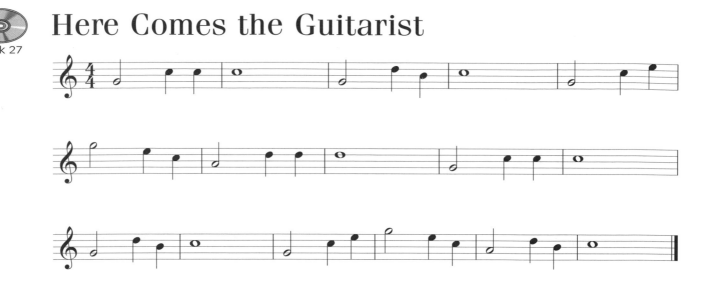

If your fingertips hurt, take a break. The more you practice, the faster they'll toughen up, but it takes time.

Track 28

Two New Notes: F♯ and C♯

Notice that we skipped the second fret on both the first and second strings. Let's go back and grab those notes.

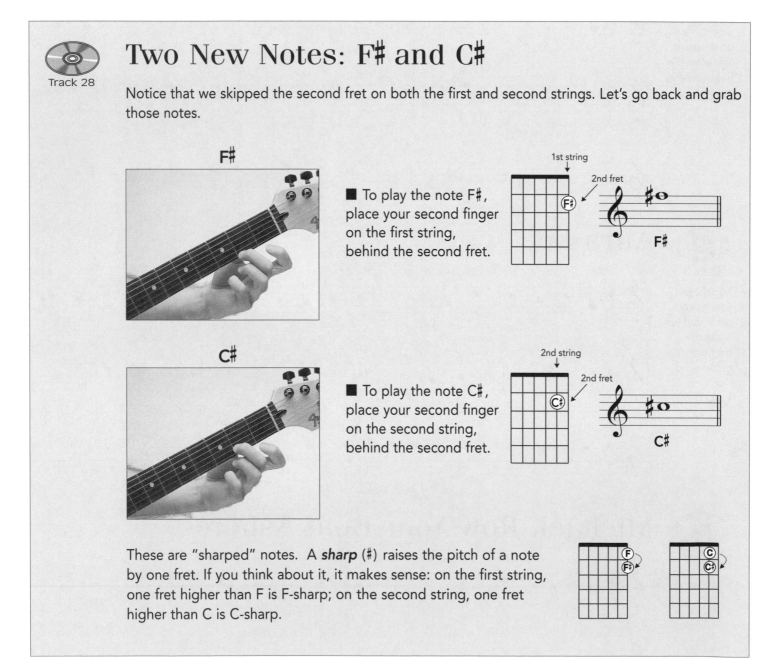

F♯

■ To play the note F♯, place your second finger on the first string, behind the second fret.

1st string

2nd fret

F♯

C♯

■ To play the note C♯, place your second finger on the second string, behind the second fret.

2nd string

2nd fret

C♯

These are "sharped" notes. A *sharp* (♯) raises the pitch of a note by one fret. If you think about it, it makes sense: on the first string, one fret higher than F is F-sharp; on the second string, one fret higher than C is C-sharp.

16

Sharps, Flats, and Naturals

Sharps are part of a group of musical symbols called **accidentals**, which raise or lower the pitch of a note:

A **sharp** (♯) raises the pitch of a note by one fret.

A **flat** (♭) lowers the pitch of a note by one fret.

A **natural** (♮) cancels a previous sharp or flat, returning a note to its original pitch.

In musical terms, the distance of one fret is called a **half step**. When a song requires a note to be a half step higher or lower, you'll see a sharp (♯), flat (♭), or natural (♮) sign in front of it. This tells you to raise or lower the note *for that measure only*. We'll see more of these "accidentals" as we continue learning more notes on the guitar.

Sharpen Up

Track 29

► Try this short exercise with your new notes.

Rockin' Sharps

Track 30

Secret Agent Sharp

Track 31

► Once again, try to keep your eyes on the music, not your fingers.

LESSON 5 | # The Fourth String: D

Track 32

The fourth string is like the third string in that we'll skip over the first fret—but this time we'll get three notes.

D

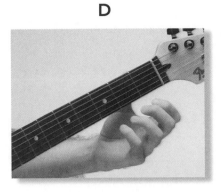

■ To play the note D, strike the open fourth string.

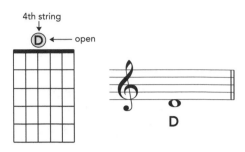

E

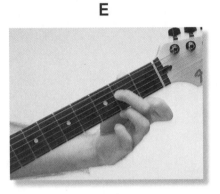

■ To play the note E, place your second finger on the fourth string, behind the second fret.

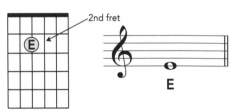

F

► Sound familiar? The new D, E, and F, sound *one octave lower* than the old D, E, and F.

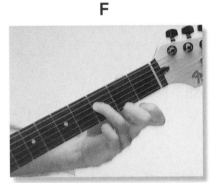

■ To play the note F, place your third finger on the fourth string, behind the third fret.

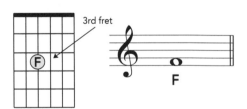

Track 33

D-E-F

Track 34

► The word *riff* is slang for a repeated instrumental figure, or musical idea.

D-String Riff

Now, try your new notes in some more songs. Practice them slowly at first.

Easy Does It

Track 35

Crosswalk Blues

Track 36

► If you like, let the D string ring out on this song.

Introducing Eighth Notes

If you divide a quarter note in half, what you get is an *eighth note*. An eighth note looks like a quarter note, but with a flag on it.

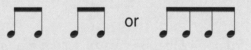

Two eighth notes equal one quarter note. To help you keep track of the beat, consecutive eighths are connected with a beam.

To count eighth notes, divide the beat into two, and use "and" between the beats. Practice this, first by counting out loud while tapping your foot on the beat, and then by playing the notes while counting and tapping.

Eighth rests are the same, but you pause instead of playing.

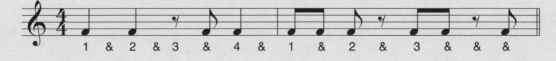

Now try some songs that use eighth notes. Keep that foot tapping!

Track 37

Alouette

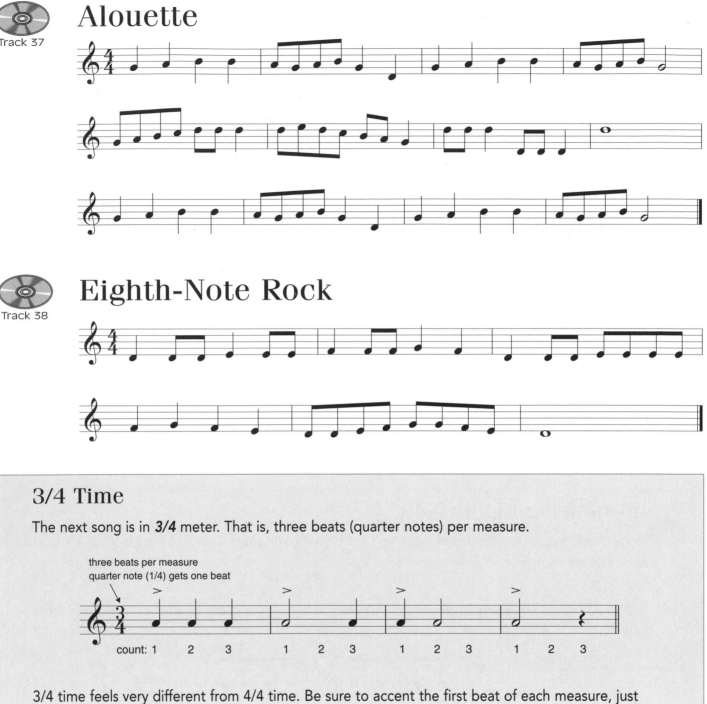

Track 38

Eighth-Note Rock

3/4 Time

The next song is in **3/4** meter. That is, three beats (quarter notes) per measure.

three beats per measure
quarter note (1/4) gets one beat

count: 1   2   3   1   2   3   1   2   3   1   2   3

3/4 time feels very different from 4/4 time. Be sure to accent the first beat of each measure, just slightly; this will help you feel the new meter.

Track 39

Amazing Grace

Two More Notes: F♯ and B♭

Track 40

From the strings that we already know, let's add two more new notes: F♯ and B♭.

F♯

■ To play the new F#, place your fourth finger on the fourth string, behind the fourth fret.

B♭

■ To play the note B♭, place your third finger on the third string, behind the third fret.

Track 41

Londonderry Air

Track 42

Snake Charmer

21

Minuet

Repeat signs ( ) tell you to repeat everything in between them. If only one sign appears (:), repeat from the beginning of the piece.

Rolling Rock

▶ Remember: A natural sign (♮) cancels an accidental on a note, returning it to its original pitch.

God Rest Ye Merry Gentlemen

Bourrée

Track 46

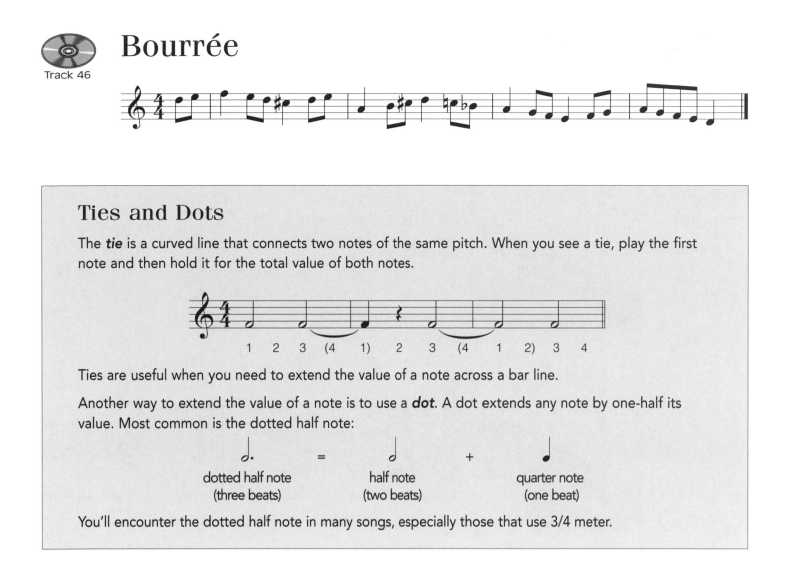

Ties and Dots

The *tie* is a curved line that connects two notes of the same pitch. When you see a tie, play the first note and then hold it for the total value of both notes.

Ties are useful when you need to extend the value of a note across a bar line.

Another way to extend the value of a note is to use a *dot*. A dot extends any note by one-half its value. Most common is the dotted half note:

dotted half note (three beats) = half note (two beats) + quarter note (one beat)

You'll encounter the dotted half note in many songs, especially those that use 3/4 meter.

It Came Upon a Midnight Clear

Track 47

23

The Fifth String: A

Track 48

Are you still in tune? Then it's time for another string. Your new notes, A, B, and C, are all played on the fifth string. Notice that these notes all make use of *ledger lines*, which extend the staff downward, allowing us to notate these lower pitches.

A

► Fingering-wise, the fifth string is just like the fourth: It uses open, 2nd, and 3rd fret positions.

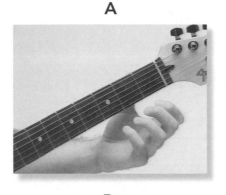

■ To play the note A, strike the open fifth string.

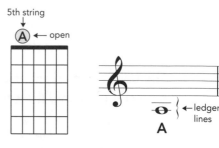

B

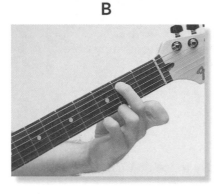

■ To play the note B, place your second finger on the fifth string, behind the second fret.

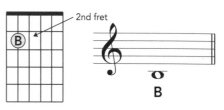

C

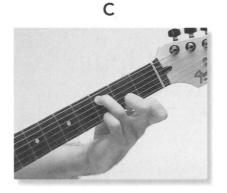

■ To play the note C, place your third finger on the fifth string, behind the third fret.

Practice your new A, B, and C. Take it slow.

Track 49

A-B-C

Cruisin'

Track 50

Track 51

Surfin'

Track 52

Fallin' Down

Track 53

Greensleeves

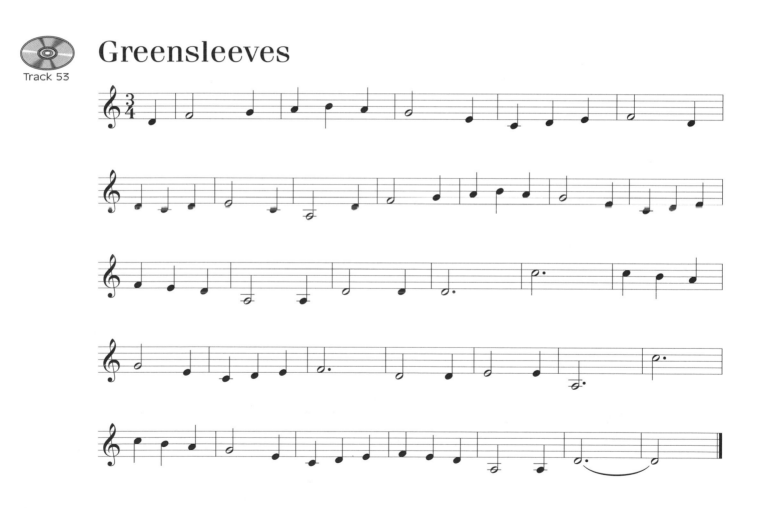

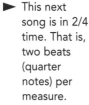

Nine Hundred Miles

► This next song is in 2/4 time. That is, two beats (quarter notes) per measure.

Introducing Alternate Picking

Alternate picking (a.k.a "the down/up stroke") is a good way of adding speed and facility to your guitar playing. It's actually a combination of two separate movements:

Downstroke Plucking or strumming the strings *downward*. This is how we've been playing all our tunes up to now. You should continue to use a downstroke for all notes that fall on a strong beat: "1," "2," "3," or "4." Remember the downstroke symbol is "⊓."

Upstroke Plucking or strumming the strings *upward*. An upstroke is generally used for an eighth note that falls on the second half of the beat—on the "and." The symbol for upstroke is "∨."

Try the following short exercises on the open high E string, using alternate picking.

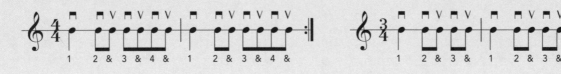

Track 55

Boogie Blues

► Now try this tune. First, play it with all downstrokes, then try the alternate picking method indicated.

LESSON 7 | # The Sixth String: E

Track 56

The notes E, F, and G are played on the sixth string of the guitar. As you practice these new notes, memorize their positions on the ledger lines.

E

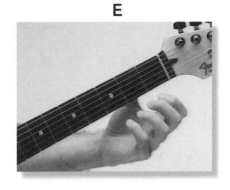

■ To play the note E, strike the open sixth string.

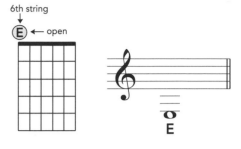

F

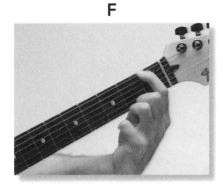

■ To play the note F, place your first finger on the sixth string, behind the first fret.

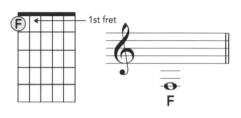

G

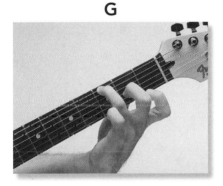

■ To play the note G, place your third finger on the sixth string, behind the third fret.

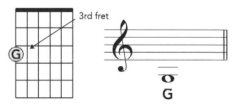

Same Notes, Different String

Notice anything familiar here? These are the exact same notes and fingerings you learned for the first string, just two octaves lower:

The trick here will be reading sind memorizing these notes on the staff. All those ledger lines can be tough. By the way, there's another set of E, F, and G notes in between the first and sixth strings. Can you find it?

27

Take it nice and slow at first. Don't forget to let your eyes read ahead of the notes you're actually playing; this can especially help on those low strings.

Sixth-String Strut

Track 57

► Try alternate picking on successive eighth notes. Stick with downstrokes for any note that occurs on the beat.

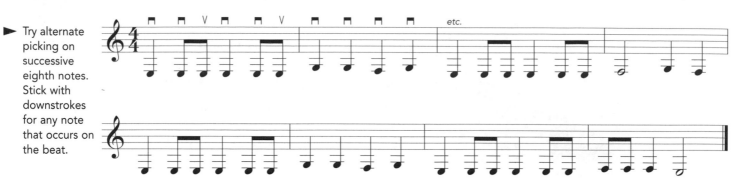

Bass Rock

Track 58

Bye Bye, Johnny

Track 59

The Dotted Quarter Note

As we know, a dot lengthens a note by one half its time value. When a quarter note is followed by a dot, its time value is increased from 1 beat to 1 1/2 beats.

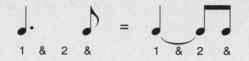

dotted quarter note   quarter note   eighth note
(1 1/2 beats)   (1 beat)   (1/2 beat)

A dotted quarter note is usually followed by an eighth note. This pattern has a total time value of two beats.

To get more comfortable with counting dotted quarter notes, try the following rhythm exercise:

Track 60

Rockin' Riff

Hark! The Herald Angels Sing

2/2 Time

In **2/2 time**, there are two beats per measure, and the half note gets the beat. This actually feels a lot like 4/4, but you only tap your foot twice in each measure.

Hail to the Guitarist

LESSON 8 | More Notes: B♭ and E♭

We may have learned all six strings, but let's double back and pick up just a few more notes before we move on.

B♭

■ To play the note B♭, place your first finger on the fifth string, behind the first fret.

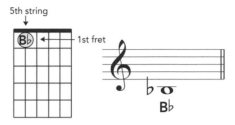

E♭

■ To play the note E♭, place your first finger on the fourth string, behind the first fret.

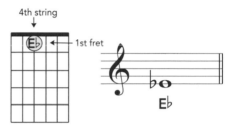

Track 64

Minor Jam

Track 65

Theme of Mystery

Track 66

Silent Night

G♯ and C♯

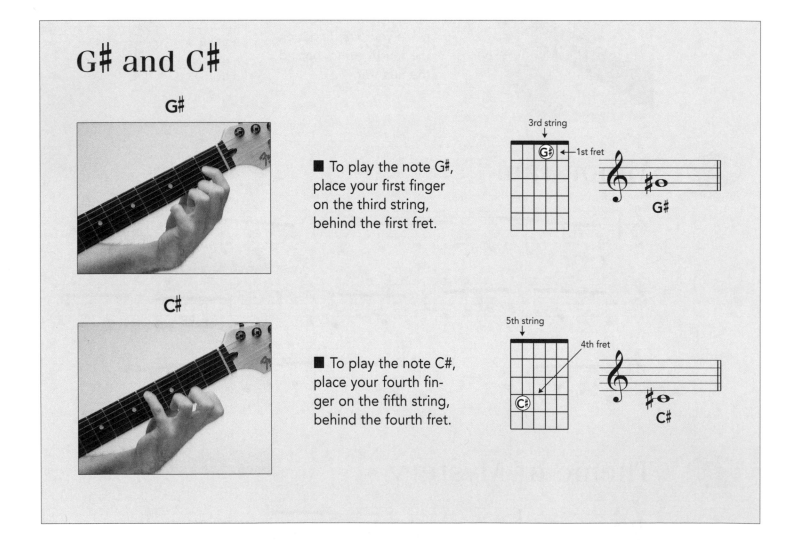

G♯

■ To play the note G♯, place your first finger on the third string, behind the first fret.

C♯

■ To play the note C♯, place your fourth finger on the fifth string, behind the fourth fret.

Track 67

Nobody Knows the Troubles I've Seen

Track 68

John Brown's Body

F♯ and G♯

These last two notes are both on the sixth string.

F♯

■ To play the note F♯, place your second finger on the sixth string, behind the second fret.

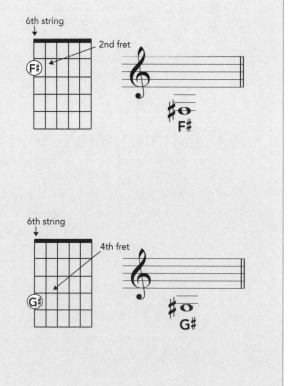

G♯

■ To play the note G♯, place your fourth finger on the sixth string, behind the fourth fret.

Blues in E

Low Groove

Track 70

► Watch the notes on this one. Try to read *ahead* of the music.

Six-String Review

We've come a long way. In fact, we've learned just about *every note* in the guitar's open position. See if you can figure out the names of the two notes that we *haven't* covered.

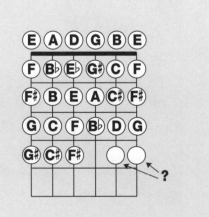

Answer: E♭, G♯

34

Major Chords

Track 71

Now that you've got a handle on all six strings, it's time to start learning about chords. *"What's a chord?"* you ask. A **chord** is three or more notes played simultaneously. We'll start off with three of the most common *major* chords. (More about what "major" means later...)

To play a chord, first get your left-hand fingers into position—the dots on each grid below tell you where to fret the strings, and the numbers tell you what fingers to use. Then, with your right hand, strum downward across the strings—but only those strings that are part of the chord. Xs above a grid tell you to avoid strumming a string. Os indicate an open string.

C

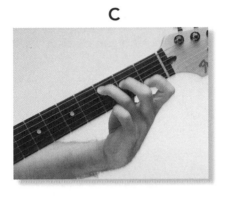

■ To play the C chord, get your fingers in place, then strum down-ward, starting on the

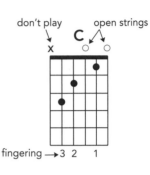

don't play   open strings

G

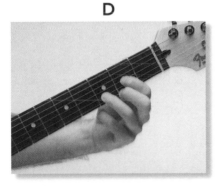

■ To play the G chord, get your fingers in place, then strum across all six strings.

D

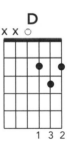

■ To play the D chord, get your fingers in place, and strum just the top four strings.

Troubleshooting Chords

If a chord sounds bad, try playing through it again, but slowly, one string at a time. If you find a "problem string," readjust your finger or your hand position, and try again.

- **Are your fingers curved?** If you let them fall flat, they'll block other strings from sounding.

- **Is your thumb on the back of the guitar neck?** This will help you apply pressure to all the strings.

- **Are your fingers directly behind the frets?** This will give you a good, clear tone.

Introducing Tablature or "TAB"

We'll be learning a new type of musical notation to go with chords called **tablature,** or **"TAB"** for short. It consists of six lines, one for each string of your guitar. The numbers written on the lines indicate which fret to play in order to sound the correct notes.

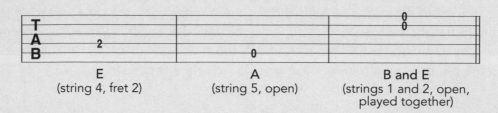

E
(string 4, fret 2)

A
(string 5, open)

B and E
(strings 1 and 2, open,
played together)

TAB is a very popular notation method for contemporary guitar music and can be used for chords *or* melodies.

Track 72

Tab This!

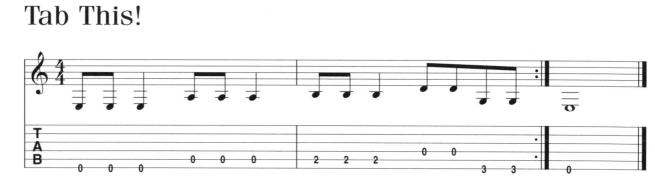

Now try reading chords in notation and TAB.

Track 73

Let's Strum

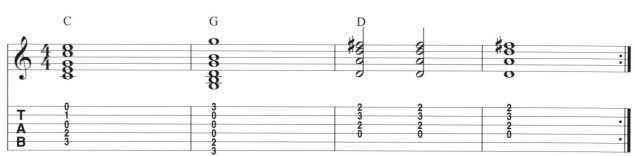

Track 74

Let's Strum, Pt. 2

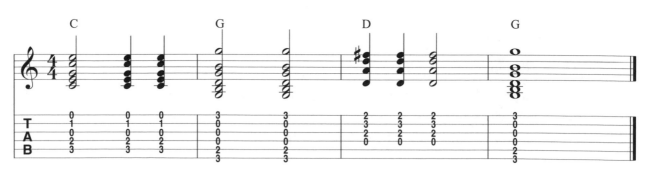

The next step is to try mixing the chords up. Chords arranged in sequence like this are called *progressions*. The number of possibilities are many. This chord progression moves from G to D to C to D and winds up back at G.

Track 75

Unplugged

► Don't be afraid to review these chords individually before playing this one!

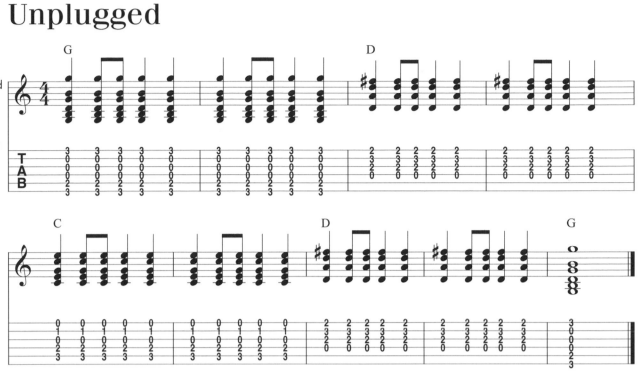

Here are a few very common progressions based on the same three chords: G, C, and D. You may recognize the first one, as it's similar to many rock songs, including "Louie, Louie" and "Wild Thing."

Track 76

Wild Rock

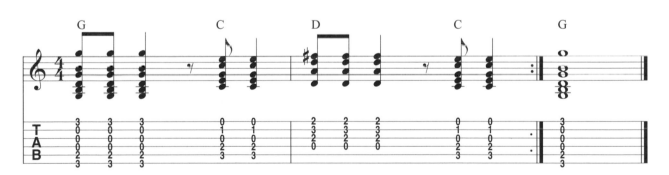

Track 77

Chord Moves

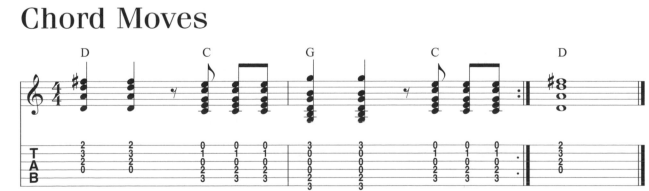

Chords can also be used to accompany a melody. Play the following songs by reading from the chord line. Strum once for each beat (that would be three strums per measure for the first two songs), and sing along with the melody.

Track 78

Good Morning to All

Track 79

Beautiful Brown Eyes

Try this: vary the number of times you strum for each chord. For example, you might want to strum along with every melody note, or just once for each measure.

This next song is in 4/4 time, so strum four times per measure—or vary your strum pattern.

Track 80

Buffalo Gals

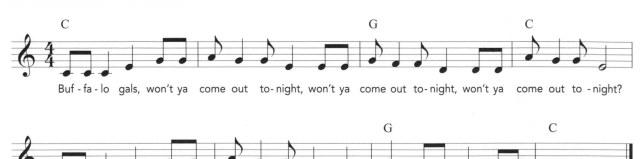

| # Minor Chords

Since we just learned three major chords, let's even things out by learning three *minor* chords.

Em

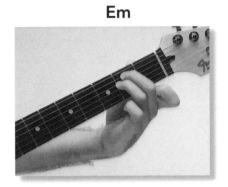

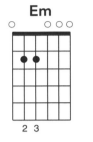

■ To play the Em chord, strum across all six strings.

Am

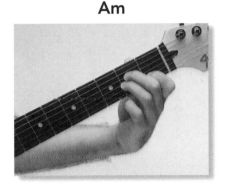

■ To play the Am, begin your strum with the fifth string.

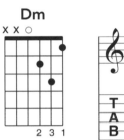

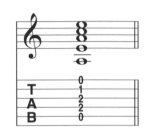

Dm

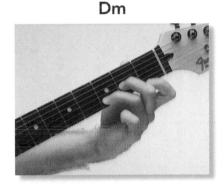

■ To play the Dm chord, strum just the top four strings.

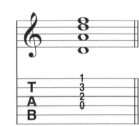

Major vs. Minor

The difference between major and minor chords is in how they sound. Take a minute to compare two major and minor chords—like D and Dm. Notice how each one makes you feel? It's difficult to put into words, but generally we say that major chords have a strong, upbeat, or happy quality, while minor chords have a darker, sadder quality.

In terms of reading them, just remember that major chords use just the letter name (e.g., D), but minor chords use letter name plus the suffix "m" (e.g., Dm).

Once again, when you feel comfortable with each chord individually, start experimenting with progressions.

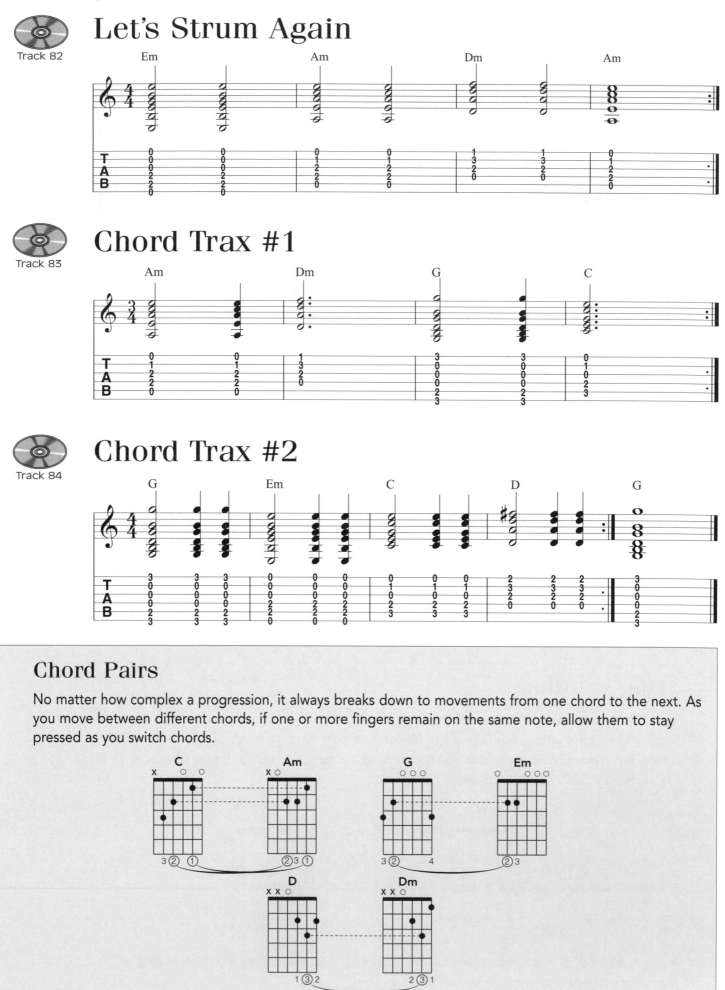

Let's Strum Again

Track 82

Chord Trax #1

Track 83

Chord Trax #2

Track 84

Chord Pairs

No matter how complex a progression, it always breaks down to movements from one chord to the next. As you move between different chords, if one or more fingers remain on the same note, allow them to stay pressed as you switch chords.

For the next example, try using an upstroke (v) for the last eighth note in each measure.

Chord Trax #3

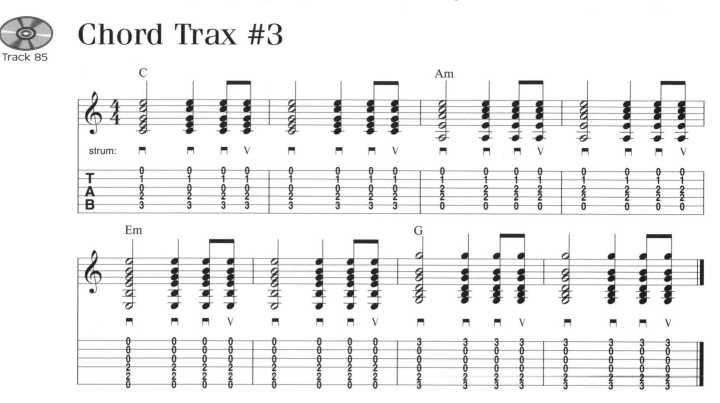

Strumming Partial Chords

When alternate strumming, don't worry about hitting every single note on the upstroke. Instead, just play two, three, or four notes of the chord—in other words, play whatever feels natural.

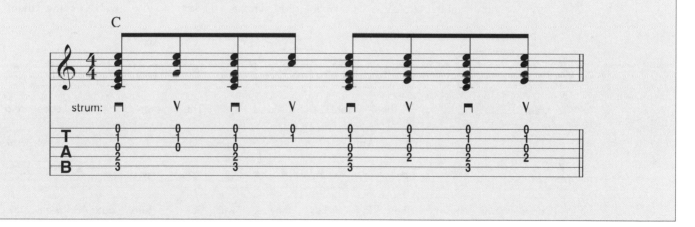

Chord Trax #4

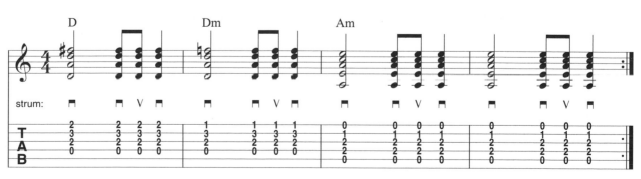

Chord Trax #5

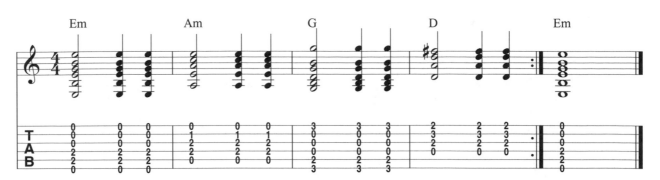

Once again, let's practice our new chords with some well-known melodies. Sing, and use the chord line to strum along.

When Johnny Comes Marching Home

When John - ny comes march - ing home a - gain hur - rah,_____ hur - rah! _____ We'll give him a heart - y wel - come then, hur - rah,_____ hur - rah! _____ The men will cheer and the boys will shout, the la - dies they_ will all turn out. And we'll all feel great when John - ny comes march - ing home. _____

Track 89

Scarborough Fair

Are you go-ing to Scar-bor-ough Fair? Pars-ley, sage, rose-ma-ry, and thyme. Re-mem-ber me to one who lives there.___ For once she was a true love of mine.

Slash Notation

Another way that you might see chord progressions written out is in **slash notation**. Slashes indicate how many beats each chord should be played; it's up to you to supply the strumming pattern. In the following progressions, first try strumming once for every slash (" / ") symbol. Then, follow the chord line and try variations of downstrokes and upstrokes.

Track 90

Makin' Trax

Practice chords daily (at least 15 minutes). Eventually, they'll become second nature. You'll instantly react when you see a chord symbol rather than trying to think of each fingering and note placement.

LESSON 11 | One More Note: A

Track 91

Let's go back to that first string and grab one more note, the high A. This one will be played with the pinky.

A

■ To play the high A, place your fourth finger on the first string, behind the fifth fret.

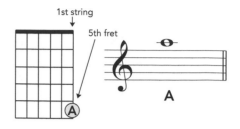

You'll probably want to move your hand up the fretboard, just a bit, to reach that fifth fret. Otherwise, you can opt to keep your hand in place, and stretch to reach the note. It's your choice.

Track 92

Hittin' the High A

From A to A to A

Now practice high A with the following scale:

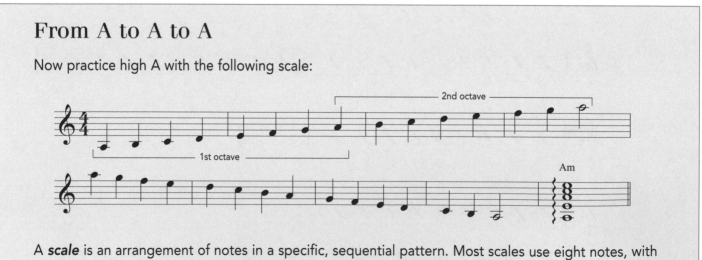

A *scale* is an arrangement of notes in a specific, sequential pattern. Most scales use eight notes, with the top and the bottom notes being an octave apart. The one above spans two octaves.

And now a few more familiar tunes.

Track 93

Home Sweet Home

Track 94

Auld Lang Syne

Track 95

House of the Rising Sun

Power Chords

Finally, let's learn one more type of chord: the **power chord**. Each of these chords uses just two strings: one open and one fretted. Also, notice that power chords are labeled with the suffix "5."

E5

■ To play the E5 chord, think: sixth string, open, and fifth string, second fret.

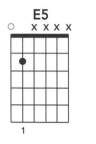
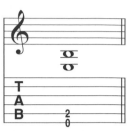

A5

■ To play the A5 chord, think: fifth string, open, and fourth string, second fret.

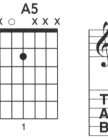

D5

■ To play the D5 chord, think: fourth string, open, and third string, second fret.

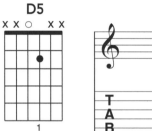

Keep It Clean

Since these chords use just two strings at a time, they don't require a full strumming motion; just enough movement to pick the two strings. To keep any upper strings from accidentally sounding when playing these chords, try letting your left-hand fretting finger lay a little bit flat, so that it touches the string(s) above lightly.

Warmin' Up

Track 97

Feelin' Good

Track 98

TIP: With each chord change, as you move your left hand down one string, move your right hand down one string at the same time.

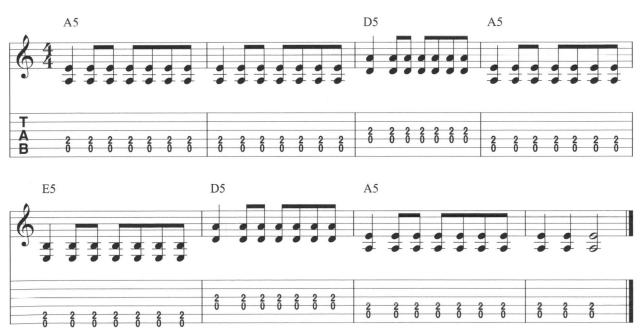

Movin' and Shakin'

Track 99

Review

Notes in First Position

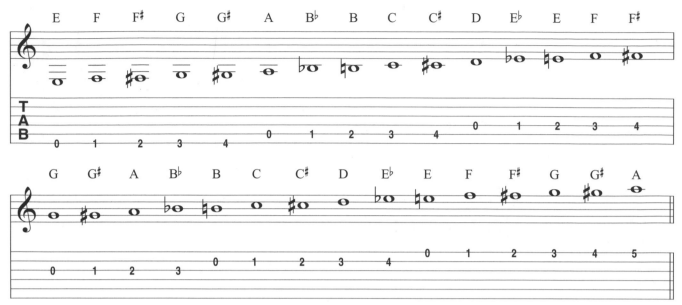

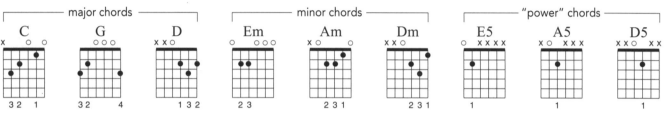

Chords

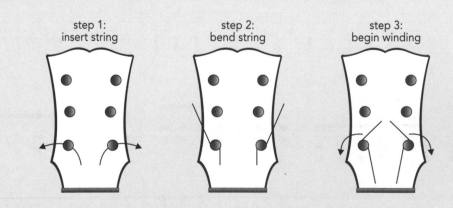

How to Change a String

If you're missing a string, or your strings are old and dirty and need replacing, you'll need to know how to change a string. The diagram below should help. Once you've inserted the string at the bridge, you need to wrap the other end around the tuning peg at the headstock. To do this, first insert the string through the posthole. Then, bend it sharply to hold the string in place, and begin winding. You should allow enough slack at the start to wrap the string completely around the peg 3-4 times, and cut off any excess when you're finished.

step 1:
insert string

step 2:
bend string

step 3:
begin winding

Keep in mind, new strings need to be "stretched out" before you can expect them to hold their pitch. You can do this by pulling on each string one at a time with your fingers (over the pickups or soundhole, away from your body) after you've strung up your guitar, then retuning each of them to the correct pitch. Repeat this until each string stays in tune even after you've pulled on it.